First Steps in Rational Emotive Behaviour Therapy

First Steps in Rational Emotive Behaviour Therapy

A Guide to Practising REBT in Peer Counselling

Second Edition

Windy Dryden

Rationality Publications

Rationality Publications
136 Montagu Mansions, London W1U 6LQ

www.rationalitypublications.com
info@rationalitypublications.com

Second edition published by Rationality Publications
Copyright (c) 2025 Windy Dryden

First edition published by the Albert Ellis Institute in 2006

A catalogue record of this book is
available from the British Library.

Second edition 2025

ISBN: 978-1-914938-42-9

Contents

Introduction

This is perhaps one of the most important books I have written on REBT. Quite a bold statement, I hear you say. So why do I make it? Let me explain.

Every year, I serve as a core trainer in the Albert Ellis Institute's Primary Certificate course training practicum, which is AEI's entry-level training programme. Of my duties, I particularly enjoy supervising trainees' initial attempts to practise REBT on this course. It is an important course since if trainees find their early attempts to practise REBT rewarding, they are more likely to seek further training in REBT than if these initial efforts are unproductive.

Very early in the course, participants are expected to practise REBT with one another and to do so in front of a small group of their peers and a supervisor who will offer them feedback either as they proceed and/or at the end of the peer counselling session. It is important to note that the person occupying the role of client in such sessions is expected to discuss a genuine current emotional problem, one for which they would genuinely like help.

So, this book is for you if you have to practise REBT in peer counselling. It has a modest but very important aim: to provide you with a simple roadmap when using REBT. As I have a specific aim, I only briefly cover REBT theory here since more detailed coverage is available in many other texts (e.g. Dryden, 2025).

Since this guide is a roadmap, I strongly suggest you use it as such, particularly if you get lost or stuck. Thus, please have this guide open when you are doing peer counselling. To make this book easy to consult while you are doing peer counselling, I have presented the material in the form of a number of points to consider.

Before I present these points, I will do two things. First, I will outline REBT's *Situational ABC* framework in brief form. Second, I will make several brief suggestions concerning your therapeutic style while you are taking the role of REBT therapist in peer counselling.

Reference

Dryden, W. (2025). *Good Practice in Rational Emotive Behaviour Therapy. 2nd edition.* Routledge.

Windy Dryden
London & Eastbourne, December 2024

REBT's *Situational ABC* Framework

The practice of Rational Emotive Behaviour Therapy is based on an understanding of people's disturbed and healthy responses to life's adversities. This is known as the *Situational ABC* framework and is particularly relevant to the practice of REBT in peer counselling, where the therapist is encouraged to work with a specific example of the client's nominated problem.[1]

As noted above, the *Situational ABC* framework provides an explanation for both your client's disturbed response (*C*) to an adversity (*A*) in a specific *Situation* and their potential healthy response (*C*) to the same adversity (*A*). What determines this response is the basic attitude (*B*) that your client holds towards the adversity: rigid/extreme in the case of a disturbed response to the adversity; flexible/non-extreme in the case of a healthy response to the same adversity. This is shown in Table 1 (see next page).[2]

I will use this framework in outlining the five steps you need to take while being an REBT therapist in peer counselling.

---

[1] I refer to the problem that the client chooses to discuss in peer counselling and the nominated problem.

[2] I will expand on each element of this framework at the appropriate place in the book.

Table 1 REBT's *Situational ABC* Framework
explaining psychological disturbance and health

Situation (Where the specific example of your client's nominated problem took place)	
Adversity (A) (The aspect of the *Situation* to which your client responded in a disturbed way and to which they could respond healthily)	
Rigid/Extreme Attitude	Flexible/Non-Extreme Attitude
• Rigid Attitude ↓	• Flexible Attitude ↓
• Awfulising Attitude	• Non-Awfulising Attitude
• Unbearability Attitude	• Bearability Attitude
• Devaluation Attitude	• Unconditional Acceptance Attitude
Unhealthy Negative Emotion and Unconstructive Behaviour	Healthy Negative Emotion and Constructive Behaviour

The Do's and Don'ts of Practising REBT in Peer Counselling

Assuming the role of an REBT therapist in a peer counselling session differs from conducting REBT in regular therapy. You have limited time to help your client as an REBT therapist in peer counselling. Depending on the number of people in your supervision group, you may have about 30 minutes to help your client. As such, I suggest that you follow several do's and don'ts.

The Do's of Practising REBT in Peer Counselling

I suggest that you do the following in your peer counselling session.

- **Be problem-focused from the outset**
  You do not have time in a short peer counselling session to do anything but be focused on the client's problem. Asking them, 'What problem can I help you with?' is a good place to start.[3]

- **Encourage the client to be as specific as possible**
  You will help your client the most in REBT peer counselling if you encourage them to select a specific example of the

---

[3] The problem that the client selects is called the 'nominated' problem.

11

nominated problem. Guard against moving from the specific to the general during the session.

- **Be active-directive**

  REBT is an active-directive approach to therapy. You are active in directing the client and yourself to understand the client's nominated problem and to deal with it in ways that encourage the client to be as active as possible.

- **Engage the client**

  REBT is best seen as a conversational approach to therapy guided by your application of the *Situational ABC* framework. Engage the client in this conversation and avoid lengthy periods of didacticism.

- **Assess the client's nominated problem using REBT's** *Situational ABC* **framework**

  REBT's *Situational ABC* framework is a key tool designed to help you undertake an assessment of the client's nominated problem. Waste no time in applying this framework to this problem.

- **Use the *Situational ABC* framework to agree on a goal with the client**

  You can also use the *Situational ABC* framework to agree on a goal related to the client's problem. Ensure that the goal helps the client to deal effectively with the adversity about which they have disturbed themself.

- **Whenever practical, explain what you are doing**

  Without being obsessive, explain to your client what you are doing at key points in the session. This helps the client to remain engaged with you.

- **Help the client stay focused in the session**

  Once your client has nominated a problem, helping the client address this problem effectively constitutes the focus of the session. Ensure that you both stay with this focus.

- **Interrupt the client when appropriate, but do so with tact**

  To help the client stay focused on their nominated problem, you may need to interrupt them. The best way of doing so is to provide a rationale for interrupting them, ask for their permission to interrupt them and encourage them to tell you the best way of doing so.

- **Make sure that your client answers the questions you ask them**

  In REBT, we ask a lot of questions. So, when asking your client an important question, ensure they answer it. If they don't, ask the question again but differently.

- **Give your client time to answer your questions**

  Another important point to remember when asking your client questions is that it is important that you give them time to answer. Otherwise, you will overload them and may end up confusing them.

- **Check out your client's understanding of your substantive points**

  REBT has a lot of concepts, and part of your skill as an REBT therapist is concerned with how accurately you convey these concepts to your client. You can only tell if your client understands the concepts you introduce to them to check their understanding. If you don't, your client may get the wrong idea about REBT concepts and respond negatively.

- **Identify and respond to your client's doubts, reservations and objections, including those that may be expressed non-verbally**
  If you have accurately conveyed REBT concepts to your client, they may still have doubts, reservations or objections (DROs) to these concepts. Ensure you encourage your clients to voice their DROs and respond to them accordingly.

The Don'ts of Practising REBT in Peer Counselling

I suggest that you avoid doing the following in your peer counselling session.

- **Don't let your client talk in an unfocused, general way**
  Many therapists have been trained to let clients talk in their own way at the beginning of therapy. This often means that your client's talk will be general and unfocused. Remember that you only have about 30 minutes to work with your client in peer counselling, and you just don't have time to work in any way that is not specific and focused. So, be specific and focused at the outset and throughout the session.

- **Don't rush your client**
  While 30 minutes may seem short, it is longer than you think, so there is no need to rush in peer counselling. As in other

areas of life, in REBT peer counselling, remember this maxim: more haste, less speed.

- **Don't be aggressive in your interventions**
  Some people who see REBT therapists do live therapy demonstrations assume wrongly that the therapist has an aggressive style of intervention and seek to emulate this style as a therapist in peer counselling. This is not a good idea. Use REBT in your own therapeutic style and resist the temptation to be aggressive. It is rarely therapeutic in any approach to therapy.

- **Don't assume that your client knows what you are doing or why you are doing it**
  Even though your client is on the same REBT course as you, don't assume that when they are in the client role, they understand what you are doing and why you are doing it. Explain your interventions and their purpose whenever possible.

- **Don't ask multiple questions**
  Some therapists in peer counselling are not tolerant of silences in peer counselling. For example, if the client does not answer a question immediately, they ask it repeatedly, thinking such repetition will bring clarity. It won't, but it will bring confusion. So, refrain from asking multiple questions.

STEP 1

Define the Problem and Be Goal-Oriented

One of the first tasks you have in peer counselling is to find out which problem your client has that they are seeking help for and what they hope to gain from discussing it with you. As you have no time to waste in peer counselling, you need to get down to work immediately.

1.1 Ask the client for a problem at the very beginning of the session

What problem would you like to focus on today?[4]

1.2 If the client mentions more than one problem, ask them to select *one*

Which of these problems do you want to select to work on?

---

[4] All questions in this guide are illustrative rather than definitive. Thus, here, you could also ask your client, 'What problem would you like to discuss with me today?'

16

The selected problem is known as the 'nominated' problem, as it is the problem that your client nominates for discussion.

1.3 Help the client to define their nominated problem

If your client talks about their nominated problem in general terms, use the information they give you to define it. Include, if possible, the adversity at *A* and their unhealthy negative emotion and, if relevant, their dysfunctional behaviour at *C*.

I get .... *C* whenever .... *A*

For example,

- *I get anxious (emotional C) when I think I may be criticised (A) and I withdraw from the Situation before it happens if I can (behavioural C)*

If your client gives you a specific example, then proceed to Step 2 unless they have a meta-emotional problem (see next point).

1.4 Assess for the presence of a meta-emotional problem and decide with the client if this is to become the nominated problem

Having disturbed themselves in the first place, human beings have the unique capacity to disturb themselves about their original disturbances. So, when your client has nominated an emotional problem (problem 1), you need to assess for the existence of what REBT therapists call their meta-emotional problem (literally an emotional problem about an emotional problem or a behavioural problem – problem 2).

How do you feel about... (state the client's original emotional/behavioural problem)?

For example:

- *When you get anxious about being criticised, how do you feel about feeling anxious?*

If your client does have a meta-emotional problem, you both need to decide which of their two problems – their original emotional/behavioural problem (problem 1) or their meta-emotional problem (problem 2) – will be their nominated problem, the one that will become the focus of the peer counselling session.

In the context of peer counselling, my advice is that you suggest to your client that you both focus on their original emotional/behavioural problem unless:

- The client wants to work on their meta-emotional problem first

- The existence of the client's meta-emotional problem will interfere with them focusing on their original emotional/behavioural problem in the session
- The existence of the client's meta-emotional problem will interfere with them working on their original emotional/behavioural problem in their life.

The important point here is that you and your client agree on her nominated problem.

1.5   Establish a goal-orientation

If you have defined your client's nominated problem in general terms, you need to establish a goal-orientation with the client. In doing so, help your client see that they need to react healthily to the adversity at *A* before changing it directly. Helping your client set a general goal direction is acceptable at this point. You will help them to set specific goals later in Step 2 (see point 2.4).

What would you like to achieve from discussing this problem with me today?

If your client replies that they want to change a *Situation* or another person, explain that while you cannot accept that as a goal, you can help them change their own behaviour, which may positively impact the *Situation* or others. If your client accepts this, then you can help them understand that they need to be in a healthy frame of mind to do this effectively, and this is best achieved by dealing with their emotional problems about the *Situation* or other(s).

STEP 2

Assess a Concrete Example of the Client's Nominated Problem

2.1   Ask the client for a concrete example of the defined problem

Once you have helped your client define their problem, help them select a concrete example of this problem. Working with a concrete example will help you to identify a specific *A* and a specific *C*, which will later help you to identify a specific rigid and extreme basic attitude at *B*.

Can you give me a concrete example of this problem?

A concrete example is one that occurred (or may occur) in a specific *Situation* at a specific time with a specific person or with specific persons present.

If your client finds it difficult to select a concrete example of their nominated problem, you can suggest that they pick an example which is fresh in their mind. This example might be:

- Recent
- Vivid or
- Typical

2.2   Get a description of the *Situation*

Ask the client to describe briefly the *Situation* in which the specific problem occurred. This description should include information concerning *where* it occurred, *when* it occurred, *who* was present, and *what* happened (e.g. I was working in my home office in the afternoon when I got an email from my boss telling me that they wanted to give me feedback on my report). The *Situation* should not include any of the client's inferences, just a description that a video camera with an audio channel would show.

2.3   Identify *C*

Ask the client to identify how they felt in the *Situation* in question. Help them select one unhealthy negative emotion and, if they feel several, help them identify the main one. If appropriate, ask them to identify their main dysfunctional behavioural response in the *Situation*.

How did you feel when … (state the *Situation*)…?
For example:

- *How did you feel when your boss wanted to give you feedback on your report?*

What did you do when… (state the *Situation*)…?
For example:

- *What did you do when your boss wanted to give you feedback on your report?*

Here are a few tips when you are assessing an emotional *C*:

- If your client gives you a vague *C*, ask them to specify it.
- Ensure that your client's *C* is unhealthy. See Table 2 for a list of the nine most common unhealthy negative emotions clients present in therapy and their healthy negative emotion alternatives.

Table 2 The nine most common unhealthy negative emotions (UNEs) presented in therapy and their healthy negative emotion alternatives (HNEs)[5]

UNEs	HNEs
• Anxiety • Depression • Guilt • Shame • Hurt • Unhealthy anger • Unhealthy regret • Unhealthy jealousy • Unhealthy envy	• Concern • Sadness • Remorse • Disappointment • Sorrow • Healthy anger • Healthy regret • Healthy jealousy • Healthy envy

- If your client is in doubt, work with them so that they see that their unhealthy negative emotion is, indeed, unhealthy.
- If your client tells you how they acted in the *Situation* rather than how they felt, investigate the unhealthy negative emotion most closely associated with their

---

[5] Please note that this list reflects the terminology that I tend to use. Developing a shared language with your client on this issue is more important than employing my language. The main point to remember is that at a suitable time, you need to engage your client in a brief discussion concerning what constitutes a healthy alternative to their UNE, given that their *A* is an adversity.

behaviour. If this is not forthcoming, accept the behaviour as the client's C if it is dysfunctional.

- Elicit your client's motivation to change C.

2.4   Identify A

I distinguish between A (the adversity in the *Situation* about which your client was most disturbed) and the *Situation* in which they were disturbed. A is usually an inference, while the *Situation* is descriptive, as mentioned in Section 2.2.

The best way I have found to assess A is using *Windy's Magic Question* (WMQ). Here is how to use this method. There are two questions that you can ask:

Windy's Magic Question (WMQ)

- Step 1. Have the client focus on their disturbed C (*e.g. anxiety*)

- Step 2: Encourage the client to focus on the *Situation* in which C occurred (e.g. *Learning that the boss wants to give the person feedback on their report*)

- Step 3: Ask the client: Which ingredient could I give you to eliminate or significantly reduce C (here, *anxiety*)? (In this case, the client said: *My boss not criticising my report*). Take care that the client does not change the *Situation* (i.e. they do not say: My boss decides not to read my report)

- Step 4: The opposite is probably A (e.g. *my boss criticising my report*), but check. Ask: *So, when you were waiting to get your boss's feedback on your report, were you most anxious about him criticising it?* If not, ask the question listed in Step 3 and then the question listed above until the client confirms what they were most anxious about in the described *Situation*

You may find Table 3 (next page) useful in helping your client to identify their *A*. It lists the themes of the adversity at *A* associated with the nine unhealthy negative emotions cited above.

Once you have identified your client's *A*, it is very important that you resist any temptation to question it, even if it is obviously distorted. Encourage your client to assume that their *A* is true, albeit temporarily. This will let you identify their rigid and extreme attitudes at *B* later.

Let's assume for the moment that ... (state *A*) ... happened. It may not have happened, but let's assume, temporarily, that it did.

For example:

- *Let's assume for the moment that your boss does criticise your report. This may not happen, but let's assume, temporarily, that it does.*

2.5 Identify the client's rigid and extreme attitudes and help them to see the flexible and non-extreme alternatives to these attitudes at *B*

At this point, you need to help your client understand that their disturbed reactions at *C* are not determined by the *Situation* or by their inference at *A* but largely by their rigid and extreme attitudes at *B*. There are several methods of doing this.

Table 3 Adversities at A related to unhealthy negative emotions at C^6

Adversity at A	Unhealthy Negative Emotion at C
• Threat	• Anxiety
• Loss • Failure • Undeserved plight (to self/others)	• Depression
• Breaking your moral code • Failing to live up to your moral code • Hurting/harming someone	• Guilt
• Something highly negative has been revealed about you (or about a group with whom you identify) by you or by others • Falling very short of your ideal • Others look down on or shun you (or a group with whom you identify)	• Shame
• Someone betrays you or lets you down, and you think you do not deserve such treatment • Another is not as invested in your relationship with them as you are	• Hurt
• You or another transgresses your personal rule • Another threatens your self-esteem • Frustration	• Unhealthy Anger
• Wishing you had not taken a course of action that you took • Wishing that you had taken a course of action that you didn't take	• Unhealthy Regret
• Threat to a valued relationship • Uncertainty related to that threat	• Unhealthy Jealousy
• Others have what you value and lack	• Unhealthy Envy

---

[6] Please note that the nine healthy negative emotions listed in Table 2 also relate to the same adversities. Thus, the threat is the adversity that features in both anxiety and concern.

The one that I think is the most efficient is what I call *Windy's Review Assessment Procedure* (WRAP). It is used to assess the client's specific rigid and extreme attitudes in the example selected by the client, but it also helps the client see what their flexible and non-extreme attitudes are that will form the attitude-based solution to their problem. In using this method, I suggest that you identify the client's rigid attitude and the one extreme attitude that best accounts for their unhealthy negative emotion.

Windy's Review Assessment Procedure (WRAP)

1. Begin by saying: *Let's review what we know and what we don't know so far.*

2. Then, say: *We know three things.*

   First, we know that you were anxious (C).

   Second, we know that you were anxious about your boss criticising your report (A).

   Third, and this is an educated guess on my part, we know that it is important to you that your boss does not criticise your report. Am I correct?

   Assuming that the client confirms your hunch, note that what you have done is to identify the part of the attitude that is common to both the client's rigid attitude and alternative flexible attitude, as we will see.

---

3. Continue by saying: *Let's review what we don't know. This is where I need your help. We don't know which of two attitudes your anxiety was based on. So, when you were anxious about your mind going blank, was your anxiety based on Attitude 1: It is important to me that my boss does not criticise my report and therefore, he must not do so (Rigid attitude) or Attitude 2: It is important to me that my boss does not criticise my report, but that does not mean that he must not do so (Flexible attitude)?*

4. If necessary, help the client to understand that their *anxiety* was based on their rigid attitude if they are unsure.

5. Once the client is clear that their *anxiety* was based on their rigid attitude, make and emphasise the rigid attitude-disturbed *C* connection. Then, ask:

    Let's suppose instead that you had a strong conviction in attitude 2. How would you feel about your boss criticising your report if you strongly believed that while it is important to you that he does not criticise your report, it does not mean that he must not do so?

6. If necessary, help the client to nominate a healthy negative emotion, such as *concern*, if not immediately volunteered, and make and emphasise the flexible attitude-healthy *C* connection.

7. Ensure that the client clearly understands the differences between the two *B–C* connections.

8. Encourage the client to set *concern* as the emotional goal in this *Situation* and to see that developing conviction in their flexible attitude is the best way of achieving this goal

Once you have identified your client's rigid and flexible attitudes, you can teach them the other three extreme attitudes and their non-extreme attitude alternatives (listed in Table 1 in the section entitled REBT's *Situational ABC* Framework above), and ask them to choose the one other extreme attitude that best accounted for their unhealthy negative emotion at *C* (and by implication the alternative non-extreme attitude that will help them to achieve their goal).

STEP 3

Preparing the Client for the Attitude Examining Process

3.1 Help the client to understand that the first step to change their attitudes is to examine them

You have now identified your client's rigid/extreme attitude and its alternative flexible/non-extreme attitude and have helped them to see the connection between the former and their unhealthy negative emotion (and/or dysfunctional behaviour) at *C* and the connection between the latter and the alternative healthy negative emotion (and/or functional behaviour) at *C*.

Your next task is to help your client understand that they need to examine their two sets of attitudes to determine which set they want to develop going forward.[7] The first three points review what you did at the end of Step 2.

- State the client's two *B–C* connections

  For example:

---

[7] You will engage them in this attitude examination process in Step 4.

30

So, you can see that if you hold a rigid attitude towards the possibility of your boss criticising your report, you will be anxious, but if you hold a flexible attitude towards this, you will feel non-anxious concern.

• Ask the client for their emotional goal

For example:

Which emotion would you want to experience about this adversity?

If the client states the healthy negative emotion, proceed to the next step below. If they state the unhealthy negative emotion, explore why and proceed until their emotional goal is their HNE.

• Help the client see that they need to change their rigid/extreme attitude to achieve this goal

For example:

Given that holding a rigid attitude leads to you feel anxiety and holding a flexible attitude would lead you to feel non-anxious concern, what do you need to change to achieve your emotional goal?

Your client should reply 'my rigid/extreme attitude' in response. If not, explore their reasoning and proceed until they can see that changing their attitude is the best way forward.

- Explain that the first step in the attitude examination process involves you helping the client to examine both sets of attitudes so that they can commit to one set going forward.

For example:

The first step in this attitude change process involves me encouraging you to stand back and examine both sets of attitudes so that you can decide which set to develop going forward and the reasons for your choice. I will do this by asking you several questions about both sets of attitudes. OK? Do you have any questions before we start?

Answer any questions the client has and then proceed to Step 4.

3.2 How to respond if the client wants to change *A* and not *B*

At this point, you may find that the client may wish to change the adversity at *A* without changing their rigid/extreme attitude at *B* first. If this is the case, help them to see that the best time to change *A* is when they are *not* disturbed about *A* and that their disturbed feelings about *A* will interfere with their change attempts. Once they understand this and that the best way to be undisturbed about *A* is by holding a flexible/non-extreme attitude towards it, they are ready to engage in the attitude examination process.

Here is how to proceed if the client wants to change *A* before *B*:

Therapist: Is it best to change ..... (state *A*) when you are feeling .... (state UNE) or when you are feeling ... (state HNE)?

Client: When I feel ... (HNE)

[*Intervene appropriately if the client says UNE*]

Therapist: ... and based on what we have discussed, what do you need to change in order to feel ... (state HNE), but not ... (state HNE) about ... (state 'A')?

Client: My rigid attitude

               [*Intervene appropriately if the client gives*
               any other answer]

For example:

Therapist: *If you decide to change how your boss is*
            likely to view your report, is it best to do so
            when you are feeling anxious or when you
            are feeling non-anxious concern?

Client: *When I feel non-anxious concern.*

Therapist: *....and based on what we have discussed,*
            what do you need to change to feel non-
            anxious concern about the prospect of
            your boss criticising your report?

Client: *My rigid attitude.*

Your client is now ready to examine their attitudes.

STEP 4

Help the Client to Examine Their Attitudes

4.1 **The purpose of helping the client to examine their attitudes is for them to see that their rigid/extreme attitude is unhealthy and that their flexible/non-extreme attitude is healthy**

When you help your client examine their rigid/extreme and flexible/non-extreme attitudes, your goal is to help them see that their rigid/extreme attitude is unhealthy (false, illogical, and yielding largely poor results) and their flexible/non-extreme attitude is healthy (true, logical and yielding largely good results). These characteristics are listed in Table 4 (next page). Helping your client to strengthen their conviction in their flexible/non-extreme attitude and weaken their conviction in their rigid/extreme attitude is initiated in Step 5.

4.2 **Help the client to examine both rigid/extreme and flexible/non-extreme attitudes together**

As I said above, the purpose of helping your client examine their attitudes is to encourage them to see that their rigid/extreme attitude is unhealthy (false, illogical and yields largely poor results) and that their alternative flexible/non-extreme attitude is healthy (true, logical and yields largely good results). This is known as intellectual insight because while the client understands this point, they do not yet have deep conviction in it to the extent that it influences for the better their feelings and behaviour. This 'emotional insight' will come about in ongoing counselling, but work towards its achievement is initiated in Step 5.

Table 4   Characteristics of rigid/extreme attitudes and flexible/non-extreme attitudes

Rigid/Extreme Attitudes	Flexible/Non-Extreme Attitudes
• False • Illogical • Leads to unconstructive results	• True • Logical • Leads to constructive results

To achieve such intellectual insight, your client must examine their rigid/extreme and flexible/non-extreme attitudes. While there are several ways of doing this, in my view, the most efficient way is to help them to examine these attitudes together and I will outline this approach here.

In doing so, I suggest that you always help your client to examine their rigid and flexible attitudes (unless there is a good reason not to), as well as the *one* other extreme attitude that your client resonates with the most, together with its non-extreme attitude alternative. You do not have time to do more than this in peer counselling. The best way of doing this is to help the client examine these two sets of attitudes separately, as shown below.

---

1. Help the client examine their rigid and flexible attitudes together. Always do this unless there is a good reason not to.

2. Separately, help the client examine together the one extreme attitude with which they most resonate and its non-extreme attitude alternative

   - Their unbearability and bearability attitudes
   - Their awfulising and non-awfulising attitudes
   - Their devaluation and unconditional acceptance attitudes

---

4.3 Help the client to examine a rigid attitude and its flexible attitude alternative

Rigid Attitude	Flexible Attitude
• *I want (don't want) X to happen, and therefore it has to be the way I want it to be*	• *I want (don't want) X to happen, but it does not have to be the way I want it to be*

I recommend that you use three main questions when helping your client to examine their rigid and flexible attitudes:

- The empirical question
- The logical question and
- The pragmatic question.

Then you can ask which attitude the client wants to strengthen and which they want to weaken and why.

First, help your client focus on their rigid attitude and its flexible attitude alternative. Suggest that your client write down both attitudes side by side (as above)[8] or write them down yourself on a whiteboard (again, as above). Then, move on to the three questions. I will present them in a certain order. This order is only a guide, and other orders are fine.

4.3.1   The empirical question

Ask: *Which of the following attitudes is true and which is false and why?*

- *The client's rigid attitude:*
- *The client's flexible attitude:*

---

[8] You will, of course, be working with their specific rigid and flexible attitudes.

According to REBT theory, the only correct answer to this question is that the flexible attitude is true and the rigid attitude is false. Help your client see that:

- A rigid attitude is inconsistent with reality. For such a rigid attitude to be true the conditions that the client is rigidly demanding to be present would already have to exist when they do not. Or, as soon as the client makes their rigid demand, these demanded conditions would have to exist. Both positions are patently inconsistent with reality.
- On the other hand, a flexible attitude is true since its two component parts are true. Your client can prove that they have a particular desire and can provide reasons why they want what they want. They can also prove that they do not have to get what they desire.

If your client gives you any other answer then help them through discussion to see why their answer is incorrect and help her to accept the correct answer.

4.3.2 The logical question

Ask: *Which of the following attitudes is logical and which is illogical, and why?*

- *The client's rigid attitude:*
- *The client's flexible attitude:*

Your client needs to acknowledge that their rigid attitude is illogical while their flexible attitude is logical. Help them to see that their rigid attitude is based on the same desire as their flexible attitude, but that they transform it as follows:

> • *I want (don't want) X to happen, and therefore it has to be the way I want it to be*

Show the client that this attitude has two components. The first [I want (don't want) X to happen] is not rigid, but the second [...and therefore it has to be the way I want it to be] is rigid. As such, the client's rigid attitude isn't logical since one cannot logically derive something rigid from something that is not rigid. Use the template in Figure 1 with your client to illustrate this visually, if necessary.

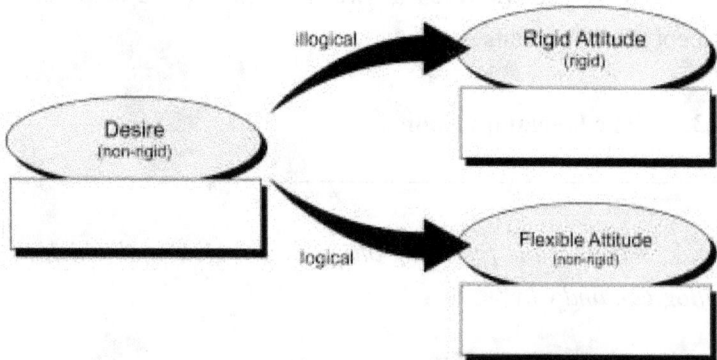

Figure 1: Examining the logical status of rigid and flexible attitudes

Your client's flexible attitude is as follows:

> • *I want (don't want) X to happen, but it does not have to be the way I want it to be*

The client's flexible attitude is logical since both parts are not rigid; thus, the second component logically follows from the first. Again, use the template in Figure 1 with your client to illustrate this visually, if necessary.

If your client gives you any other answer, then help them through discussion to see why their answer is incorrect and help them to accept the correct answer.

4.3.3　The pragmatic question

> Ask: *Which of the following attitudes leads to largely good results and which leads to largely poor results and why?*
>
> • *The client's rigid attitude:*
> • *The client's flexible attitude:*

You need to help your client acknowledge that their rigid attitude leads to largely unconstructive results, while their flexible attitude leads to more constructive ones. As you do this, use the information provided by your client when you discussed the two *B–C* connections (see point 2.5).

If your client thinks their rigid attitude leads to healthier consequences than their flexible attitude, help them through discussion to see why they are likely to be mistaken.

4.3.4   Assess the client's commitment to attitude change

At this point, you want to assess your client's commitment to change their attitude. You do this by asking the following question:

Ask: *Which attitude does the client want to strengthen, and which do they want to weaken and why?*

- *The client's rigid attitude*
- *The client's flexible attitude*

After helping your client to examine their rigid and flexible attitudes, your client 'should' indicate that they wish to work to strengthen their conviction in their flexible attitude and weaken their conviction in their rigid attitude and be able to give coherent reasons why based on their problematic feelings and behaviour and their goals for change. If your client gives you any other answer, discover the reasons for this response and work with them until they fully commit to their flexible attitude.

4.4 Help the client to examine an awfulising attitude and its non-awfulising attitude alternative

Awfulising Attitude	Non-Awfulising Attitude
• *It would be bad if X happens (or does not happen), and therefore it would be terrible*	• *It would be bad if X happens (or does not happen), but it isn't terrible*

When helping your client examine their awfulising and non-awfulising attitudes, use the same three questions you used to help them examine their rigid and flexible attitudes: empirical, logical, and pragmatic. Once you have done this, you can ask which attitude your client wants to strengthen, which they want to weaken, and why.

First, help your client focus on their awfulising attitude and non-awfulising attitude. Again, invite them to write them down side by side (as above)[9] or write them down yourself on a whiteboard (again, as above). Then, move on to the three questions.

---

[9] Again, you will be working with their specific awfulising and non-awfulising attitudes.

4.4.1　The empirical question

Ask: *Which of the following attitudes is true and which is false and why?*

- *The client's awfulising attitude:*
- *The client's non-awfulising attitude:*

According to REBT theory, an awfulising attitude is false and a non-awfulising attitude is true.

While examining these attitudes, help your client see that when they are holding their awfulising attitude, they believe the following:

- Nothing could be worse;
- The event in question is worse than 100% bad
- No good could possibly come from this bad event
- They cannot transcend the event

Help your client see that all three convictions are inconsistent with reality and that their awfulising attitude is false. By contrast, help them to see that their non-awfulising attitude is true since this is made up of the following ideas:

- Things could always be worse;
- The event in question is less than 100% bad
- Some good could come from this bad event
- They can transcend the event

If your client gives you answers that is at variance with the above, then help them through discussion to see why their answer is incorrect and help them to accept the correct answer.

4.4.2   The logical question

Ask: *Which of the following attitudes is logical and which is illogical, and why?*

- *The client's awfulising attitude:*
- *The client's non-awfulising attitude:*

Help your client see that their awfulising attitude is illogical, while their non-awfulising attitude is logical. Show them that their awfulising attitude is based on the same evaluation of badness as their non-awfulising attitude, but they transform this as follows:

It would be very bad if X happened (or did not happen) ... and therefore it would be terrible.

Show your client that their awfulising attitude has two components. The first [It would be very bad if X happened (or did not happen)] is non-extreme, while the second (...and therefore it would be terrible) is extreme. As such, help them to see that their awfulising attitude is illogical since one cannot logically derive something extreme from something that is not extreme. Use the template in Figure 2 with your client to illustrate this point visually, if necessary.

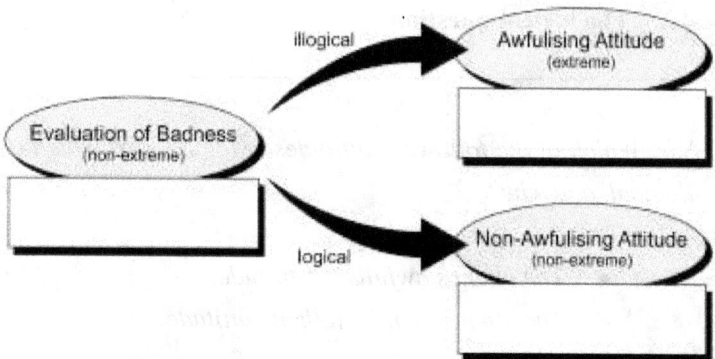

Figure 2: Examining the logical status of awfulising and non-awfulising attitudes

Your client's non-awfulising attitude is as follows:

It would be very bad if X happened (or did not happen) ... but it would not be terrible.

Encourage your client to see that their non-awfulising attitude is logical since both parts are non-extreme and thus the second component logically follows from the first. Again, use the template in Figure 2 with your client to illustrate this point visually, if necessary.

4.4.3 The pragmatic question

Ask: *Which of the following attitudes leads to largely good results and which leads to largely poor results and why?*

- *The client's awfulising attitude:*
- *The client's non-awfulising attitude:*

You need to help your client acknowledge that their awfulising attitude leads to largely unconstructive results, while their non-awfulising attitude leads to more constructive ones. As you do this, use the information provided by your client when you discussed the two *B–C* connections (see point 2.5).

If your client thinks their awfulising attitude leads to healthier consequences than their flexible attitude, help them through discussion to see why they are likely to be mistaken.

4.4.4 Assess the client's commitment to attitude change

At this point, you want to assess your client's commitment to change their attitude. You do this by asking the following question:

Ask: *Which attitude does the client want to strengthen, and which do they want to weaken and why?*

- *The client's awfulising attitude*
- *The client's non-awfulising attitude*

After helping your client to examine their awfulising and non-awfulising attitudes, your client 'should' indicate that they wish to work to strengthen their conviction in their non-awfulising attitude and weaken their conviction in their awfulising attitude and be able to give coherent reasons why based on their problematic feelings and behaviour and their goals for change. If your client gives you any other answer, discover the reasons for this response and work with them until they fully commit to their non-awfulising attitude.

4.5   Help the client to examine an unbearability attitude and its bearability attitude alternative

Unbearability Attitude	Bearability Attitude
• *It would be a struggle for me to bear it if X happens (or does not happen), and therefore I could not bear it*	• *It would be a struggle for me to bear it if X happens (or does not happen), but I could bear it. It would be worth it to me to do so, and I am worth bearing it for. I am willing to bear it, and I am going to bear it.*

When helping your client examine their unbearability and bearability attitudes, use the same three questions you used to help them examine their rigid and flexible attitudes: the empirical, logical, and pragmatic. Once you have done this, you can ask which attitude your client wants to strengthen, which they want to weaken, and why.

As before, begin by suggesting that your client focus on their unbearability attitude and their bearability attitude alternative. Encourage them to write down both attitudes side by side (as above)[10] or write them down yourself on a whiteboard (again, as above). Then, move on to the three questions.

4.5.1 The empirical question

Ask: *Which of the following attitudes is true and which is false and why?*

- *The client's unbearability attitude:*
- *The client's bearability attitude:*

According to REBT theory, an unbearability attitude is false, and a bearability attitude is true.

While examining these attitudes, help your client see that when they are holding their unbearability attitude, they believe the following:

---

[10] Yet again, you will be working with their specific unbearability and bearability attitudes.

- I will die or disintegrate if the adversity continues to exist
- I will lose the capacity to experience happiness if the adversity continues to exist.

Help your client to see that both these convictions are inconsistent with reality and that their unbearability attitude is false. By contrast, help them to see that their bearability attitude is true since this is made up of the following ideas:

- I will struggle if the adversity continues to exist, but I will neither die nor disintegrate;
- I will not lose the capacity to experience happiness if the adversity continues to exist, although this capacity will be temporarily diminished; and
- The adversity is worth bearing.
- I am worth bearing the adversity for
- I am willing to bear it
- I am going to bear it

If your client gives you an answer that is at variance with the above, then help them through discussion to see why their answer is incorrect and help them to accept the correct answer.

4.5.2 The logical question

Ask: *Which of the following attitudes is logical and which is illogical, and why?*

- *The client's unbearability attitude:*
- *The client's bearability attitude:*

Your client needs to acknowledge that their unbearability attitude is illogical while their bearability attitude is logical. Help them to see that unbearability attitude is based on the same struggle component as their bearability attitude, but that they transform it as follows:

It would be a struggle for me to bear it if X happened (or did not happen ... and therefore it would be unbearable

Show the client that this attitude has two components. The first [It would be a struggle for me to bear it if X happened (or did not happen)] is not extreme, but the second [...and therefore it would be unbearable] is extreme. As such, the client's unbearability attitude isn't logical since one cannot logically derive something extreme from something that is not extreme rigid. Use the template in Figure 3 with your client to illustrate this point visually, if necessary.

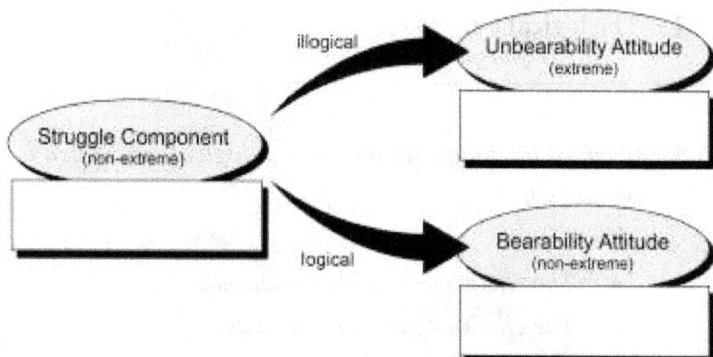

Figure 3: Examining the logical status of unbearability and bearability attitudes

Your client's bearability attitude is as follows:

> - *It would be a struggle for me to bear it if X happens (or does not happen), but I could bear it. It would be worth it to me to do so, and I am worth bearing it for. I am willing to bear it, and I am going to bear it.*

The client's bearability attitude is logical since all of its components are not extreme and are thus logically connected due to their non-extreme nature. Again, use the template in Figure 3 with your client to illustrate this visually, if necessary.

If your client gives you any other answer, then help them through discussion to see why their answer is incorrect and help them to accept the correct answer.

4.5.3   The pragmatic question

Ask: *Which of the following attitudes leads to largely good results and which leads to largely poor results and why?*

- *The client's unbearability attitude:*
- *The client's bearability attitude:*

You need to help your client acknowledge that their unbearability attitude leads to largely unconstructive results, while their bearability attitude leads to more constructive ones. As you do this, use the information provided by your client when you discussed the two *B–C* connections (see point 2.5).

If your client thinks their unbearability attitude leads to healthier consequences than their bearability attitude, help them through discussion to see why they are likely to be mistaken.

4.5.4   Assess the client's commitment to attitude change

At this point, you want to assess your client's commitment to change their attitude. You do this by asking the following question:

Ask: *Which attitude do you want to strengthen, and which do you want to weaken and why?*

After helping your client to examine their unbearability and bearability attitudes, your client 'should' indicate that they wish to work to strengthen their conviction in their bearability attitude and weaken their conviction in their unbearability attitude and be able to give coherent reasons why based on their problematic feelings and behaviour and their goals for change. If your client gives you any other answer, discover the reasons for this response and work with them until they fully commit to their bearability attitude.

4.6 Help the client to examine a devaluation attitude and its unconditional acceptance attitude alternative

Devaluation Attitude	Unconditional Acceptance Attitude
• *If X happens (or does not happen), it proves that:* - *I am no good or* - *You are no good or* - *Life is no good*	• *If X happens (or does not happen), it does not prove that:* - *I am no good or* - *You are no good or* - *Life is no good* *It proves that:* - *I am a complex, unrateable fallible human being* - *You are a complex, unrateable human being* - *Life is a complex mixture of good, bad and neutral and is thus unrateable*

When helping your client examine their devaluation and unconditional acceptance attitudes, again use the same three questions you used to help them examine their rigid and flexible attitudes: empirical, logical, and pragmatic. Once you have done this, you can ask which attitude your client wants to strengthen, which they want to weaken, and why.

Once again, begin by suggesting that your client focus on their devaluation attitude and their unconditional acceptance attitude alternative. As before, encourage your client to write down both attitudes side by side (as above)[11] or write them down yourself on a whiteboard (again, as above). Then move on to the three questions.

4.6.1   The empirical question

Ask: *Which of the following attitudes is true and which is false and why?*

- *The client's devaluation attitude:*
- *The client's unconditional acceptance attitude:*

According to REBT theory, an unconditional acceptance attitude is true, and a devaluation attitude is false.

---

[11] As before, you will be working with their specific devaluation and unconditional acceptance attitudes.

4.6.1.1 Helping your client to examine the empirical status of their person-devaluation[12] attitude and its unconditional acceptance attitude alternative

Help your client to see that when they hold a person-devaluation attitude towards themself or another person, they believe the following:

- A person (self or other) can legitimately be given a single global rating that defines their essence and the worth of a person is dependent upon conditions that change (e.g. my worth goes up when I do well and goes down when I don't do well).
- A person can be rated based on one of their aspects.

Help your client to see that these convictions are inconsistent with reality and that their person-devaluation attitude is false. By contrast, help them to see that their unconditional acceptance attitude held towards themself or another person is true since this is made up of the following ideas:

- A person cannot legitimately be given a single global rating that defines their essence and their worth, as far as they have it, is not dependent upon conditions that change (e.g. my worth stays the same whether or not I do well).
- It makes sense to rate discrete aspects of a person, but it does not make sense to rate a person based on these discrete aspects since the person is far too complex to merit such a rating.

---

[12] This may be a self-devaluation or other-devaluation attitude.

4.6.1.2 Helping your client to examine the empirical status of their life-devaluation attitude and its unconditional acceptance attitude alternative

Help your client see that when they hold a life-devaluation attitude, they believe the following:

- The world can legitimately be given a single rating that defines its essential nature and that the value of the world varies according to what happens within it (e.g. the value of the world goes up when something fair occurs and goes down when something unfair happens).
- The world can be rated based on one of its aspects.

Help your client see that these convictions are inconsistent with reality and that their life-devaluation attitude is false. By contrast, help them to see that their unconditional life-acceptance attitude is true since this is made up of the following ideas:

- Life cannot legitimately be given a single rating that defines its essential nature, and its value does not vary according to what happens within it (e.g. the value of life stays the same whether fairness exists at any given time or not).
- It makes sense to rate discrete aspects of life, but it does not make sense to rate life based on these discrete aspects since life is far to complex to merit such a rating.

If your client gives you an answer that is at variance with the above, then help them through discussion to see why their response is incorrect and help them accept the correct answer.

4.6.2 The logical question

Ask: *Which of the following attitudes is logical and which is logical and why?*

- *The client's devaluation attitude:*
- *The client's unconditional acceptance attitude:*

Help your client see that their devaluation attitude is illogical, while their unconditional acceptance attitude is logical.[13]

For example, if your client holds a self-devaluation attitude show them that this attitude is based on the same idea as their unconditional self-acceptance attitude in that in both they acknowledge that it is bad if X happened, for example, but that they transform it as follows:

X is bad… and therefore I am bad

For example:

It would be bad if my boss criticises my report and if he does it proves I am worthless.

---

[13] The points in this section also apply to a client's life-devaluation and unconditional life-acceptance attitudes.

Here, the client's self-devaluation attitude has two components. The first (X is bad...) is the client's evaluation of a part of their experience, while the second (...and therefore I am bad) is their evaluation of the whole of their *self.* As such, the client is making the illogical part–whole error where the part is deemed illogically to define the whole.

Your client's unconditional self-acceptance attitude is as follows:

X is bad, but this does not mean that I am bad. I am a fallible human being even though X happened

For example:

It would be bad if my boss criticises my report. If he does, it does not prove I am worthless. I am the same unrateable, complex fallible human being whether he criticises my report or not.

Encourage your client to see that their unconditional self-acceptance attitude is logical because it shows that their *self* is complex and incorporates a bad event. Thus, in holding their unconditional self-acceptance attitude, the client avoids making the part-whole error.

4.6.3 The pragmatic question

Ask: *Which of the following attitudes leads to largely good results and which leads to largely poor results and why?*

- *The client's devaluation attitude:*
- *The client's unconditional acceptance attitude:*

You need to help your client acknowledge that their devaluation attitude leads to largely unconstructive results, while their unconditional acceptance attitude leads to more constructive ones. As you do this, use the information provided by your client when you discussed the two *B–C* connections (see point 2.5).

If your client thinks their devaluation attitude leads to healthier consequences than their unconditional acceptance attitude, help them through discussion to see why they are likely to be mistaken.

4.6.4 Assess the client's commitment to attitude change

At this point, you want to assess your client's commitment to change their attitude. You do this by asking the following question:

Ask: *Which attitude do you want to strengthen, and which do you want to weaken and why?*

After helping your client to examine their devaluation and unconditional acceptance attitudes, your client 'should' indicate that they wish to work to strengthen their conviction in their unconditional acceptance attitude and weaken their conviction in their devaluation attitude and be able to give coherent reasons why based on their problematic feelings and behaviour and their goals for change. If your client gives you any other answer, discover the reasons for this response and work with them until they fully commit to their unconditional acceptance attitude.

STEP 5

Help the Client to Strengthen Their Conviction in their Flexible/Non-Extreme Attitude and Weaken Their Conviction in Their Rigid/Extreme Attitude

While a full discussion of how to help your client strengthen their conviction in their flexible/non-extreme attitude and weaken their conviction in their rigid/extreme attitude is beyond the scope of this book, I will suggest two ways to encourage your client to initiate this process.

5.1 Use rational-emotive imagery in the session and suggest it for homework

Rational-emotive imagery (REI) is an imagery method designed to help your client practise changing their *specific* rigid/extreme attitude to its flexible/non-extreme alternative while they simultaneously imagine the adversity in the specific *Situation* in question. Help your client to understand that this method will help them to strengthen their conviction in their new flexible/non-extreme attitude and weaken their conviction in their rigid/extreme attitude.

What follows is a set of instructions for using Albert Ellis's version of REI.

5.1.1 Instructions for using REI: Ellis version

- Encourage your client to take a *Situation* in which they disturbed themself and identify the aspect of the *Situation* they were most disturbed about. This is the adversity at *A*.
- Ask your client to close their eyes and imagine the *Situation* as vividly as possible, and focus intently on the adversity.
- Encourage your client to really experience the unhealthy negative emotion that they felt at the time while still focusing intently on the adversity. Ensure that the client's unhealthy negative emotion is *one* of the following: anxiety, depression, shame, guilt, hurt, unhealthy anger, unhealthy regret, unhealthy jealousy or unhealthy envy.
- Encourage them to really experience this disturbed emotion for a moment or two and then change their emotional response to a healthy negative emotion while continuing to focus intently on the adversity. Encourage them *not* to change the intensity of the emotion, just the emotion. Thus, if their original unhealthy negative emotion was anxiety, encourage them to change this to concern; if it was depression, encourage them to change it to sadness. Suggest that they change shame to disappointment, guilt to remorse, hurt to sorrow, unhealthy anger to healthy anger, unhealthy regret to healthy regret, unhealthy jealousy to healthy jealousy and unhealthy envy to healthy envy. Stress that they should change the unhealthy negative emotion to its healthy equivalent but keep the level of intensity of the

new emotion as strong as the old emotion. Encourage them to keep experiencing this new emotion for about five minutes, all the time focusing keenly on the adversity. If your client goes back to the old, unhealthy negative emotion, encourage them to bring the new, healthy negative emotion back.

- At the end of five minutes, ask your client how their changed their emotion.
- Ensure that they changed their emotional response by changing their specific rigid/extreme attitude to its flexible/non-extreme alternative. If they did not do so (if, for example, they changed their emotion by changing the adversity to make it less negative or neutral or by holding an indifference attitude towards the adversity), suggest that they do the exercise again and keep doing this until they have changed their emotion only by changing their specific rigid/extreme attitude to its flexible/non-extreme attitude alternative.

Encourage your client to practise REI several times a day and suggest that they aim for 30 minutes daily practice when they are not doing any other therapy homework.

5.2 Suggest for homework that the client rehearses their flexible/non-extreme attitude while acting in ways that are consistent with this attitude

Perhaps the most powerful way of helping your client to strengthen their flexible/non-extreme attitude is to encourage them to rehearse it while facing the relevant adversity at *A* and while acting in ways that are consistent with this flexible/non-extreme attitude.

Thus, end the peer counselling session, if you can, by negotiating a homework assignment that helps your client to implement the above principle and is based on the work that the two of you have done in the session.

If you need to, help your client to see that when their behaviour and flexible/non-extreme attitude are in sync and they keep them in sync, they maximise the chances of strengthening their conviction in this attitude. Conversely, discourage your client from acting in ways consistent with her old rigid/extreme attitude. Otherwise, they will make limited progress in changing their attitude.

Keep the following in mind reminder when negotiating the homework task with your client and suggest that the client uses it for themselves going forward.

Face the adversity at *A* + Rehearse the flexible/non-extreme attitude at *B* + Act in ways consistent with this flexible/non-extreme attitude.

You have now reached the end of this guide. I would appreciate receiving feedback on your experiences using it during peer counselling so that I may improve subsequent editions. Feel free to email me your comments at windy@windydryden.com

Index